by Darwyn Lyles

SCHOOL PUBLISHERS

Cover, p.6–7, ©Ariel Skelley/CORBIS; p.3, p.12, ©Thinkstock/Alamy; p.4, ©Big Cheese Photo LLC/ Alamy; p.5, ©Laura Dwight/PhotoEdit; p.8, ©Corbis; p.9, ©Roy Morsch/CORBIS; p.10, ©Hein van den Heuvel/zefa/Corbis; p.11, ©Michael Newman/PhotoEdit; p.13, (b) ©chicagoview/Alamy, (t) ©Joseph Sohm; ChromoSohm Inc./CORBIS; p.14, ©Corbis/PunchStock.

Printed in China

ISBN 10: 0-15-350180-4
ISBN 13: 978-0-15-350180-7

Ordering Options
ISBN 10: 0-15-349939-7 (Grade 4 ELL Collection)
ISBN 13: 978-0-15-349939-5 (Grade 4 ELL Collection)
ISBN 10: 0-15-357279-5 (package of 5)
ISBN 13: 978-0-15-357279-1 (package of 5)

2 3 4 5 6 7 8 9 10 985 12 11 10 09 08 07

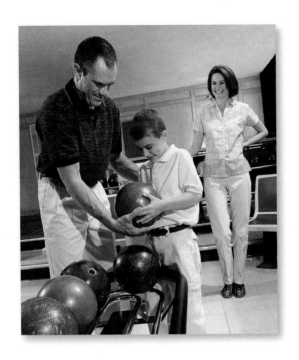

John's family goes bowling every Friday night in the winter. The family has fun at the bowling alley. John always looks forward to bowling when winter comes. Bowling on Friday nights is a family tradition.

Children learn traditions from their families. Some day John may have his own children. He may take his children bowling on Friday nights. He will preserve, or continue, the tradition in this way.

Traditions help family members bond. To bond means to feel close to one another.

Many families celebrate when a baby is born. It is an exciting time. Family members often visit the mother. Family members often hold the new baby.

Some family members give the baby a gift. For example, they may give the baby clothes or a toy. Some family members may knit something for the baby out of yarn. Some aunts knit the new baby a blanket. The aunts may also knit the baby some slippers.

Have you ever seen a quilt? A quilt is a padded blanket usually made in many different colors. Quilts are often heavy and warm. Some people sew their own quilts. The people give the quilts interesting designs.

Many people make quilts for others. For example, a grandmother may sew a quilt for each of her grandchildren. She may give each grandchild a quilt on his or her first birthday. The birthday quilt is a tradition in the family.

Food is part of many family traditions. Some families have a big meal on Sunday. They have the meal in the afternoon. The Sunday afternoon meal is usually special. A family may eat a turkey dinner. An adult family member puts the turkey in the oven in the morning. It smells delicious. By afternoon, the turkey is ready to eat. Then the family sits at the table. The family members eat the turkey and other foods. The family members talk and tell stories. They eat some more. The dinner is a nice tradition.

There are other traditions that include food. Some families have special birthday meals. If a child is having a birthday, a family member may cook the child's favorite dish. Some children may want pasta. Some children may want chicken and vegetables. The whole family sits at the table and enjoys the meal together. When it is time for dessert, the family may have birthday cake and sing to the child.

Many families have summer traditions. Some families go on vacation. They may go to the same cabin in the woods every year. They may go to another state. They may visit a fun place. Some families go to the beach each summer. They swim in the water. They walk along the beach. They play in the sand.

Adults often take pictures on these trips. Later, family members may look at the pictures and remember the fun times. The family members have good memories of their summer tradition.

Have you ever been to a family reunion? A family reunion is when family members get together to visit with one another. They have a large picnic or party. Many family members travel a long way to get to the reunion. They may come from other cities or states.

Family members often play games at the reunion. They may play volleyball or horseshoes. Family members talk to one another. They share stories about their lives.

Families have autumn traditions. Autumn is the season when leaves fall off many trees. Some families pick apples each autumn. Apples get ripe in autumn. They are not too hard or too soft. The apples are ready to be eaten.

Some families pick apples at an orchard. An orchard is a place where fruit trees grow. The family members pick apples from the trees and place the apples in baskets. The family members take the apples home. Some families make apple pies. Other families just eat up the apples!

Raking leaves is another autumn tradition. Family members work together to rake the leaves around the house into piles. Sometimes the children jump into the piles! The children do not get hurt because the leaves are soft. It is fun to play in leaves. The family members play in the leaves for a while. They rake the leaves up again when the fun is over. Then the trash collector may come and take the leaves away.

Some families decorate the outsides of their homes each autumn. The families may use pumpkins. Have you ever carved a pumpkin? Families also decorate with dried cornstalks. Corn once grew on the cornstalks. The cornstalks are tall and thin. A family may place a bunch of cornstalks in front of the house. Some families decorate with squash. Squash are colorful fall vegetables. Family members may put a basket of squash on the front porch.

Have you ever gone to a parade? People enjoy going to parades. Many families go to a parade each year at the same time. People like seeing the marching bands play music. Family members cheer. They wave to people who walk by. They look at the fancy cars. Sometimes important community leaders march in the parade. It is fun to see these leaders in person. People at parades often take pictures of what they see.

Many people have family portraits taken each year. A family portrait is a photograph of the whole family. The family members meet in a special place. The photographer tells the family members where to stand. Then the photographer takes a picture of the whole family. Smile!

Families do things together. They have fun together. They make traditions together.

Scaffolded Language Development

VERB CONJUGATION Remind students that a verb may take a different form depending on the subject. Write the conjugation for the verb *to laugh* on the board: *I laugh, you laugh, he/she laughs, we laugh, they laugh.* Read aloud the conjugation, and point out how the verb changes for the subjects *he* and *she.* Divide the group into two teams. Write the verbs below on slips of paper, and place them face down in a pile. Have one student from the first team take a slip. The team must discuss and conjugate the verb chorally. If the verb is conjugated correctly, the team gets a point. Then it is the second team's turn.

to play	to go
to march	to grow
to decorate	to be
to enjoy	to have

 Art

Draw a Picture Have students draw a picture of one of the traditions shown in this book. Then have them write a sentence that explains what their drawing shows.

School-Home Connection

Preserving Family Traditions Ask students to discuss this story with an older family member. Then have them discuss some of their family traditions and how they may have begun.

Word Count: 933